AIRSTREAM
THE SILVER RV

Tara Cox

SHIRE PUBLICATIONS

Published in Great Britain in 2013 by Shire Publications Ltd, Midland House, West Way, Botley, Oxford OX2 0PH, United Kingdom.

43-01 21st Street, Suite 220B, Long Island City, NY 11101, USA.

E-mail: shire@shirebooks.co.uk www.shirebooks.co.uk

A CIP catalog record for this book is available from the British Library.

Shire Library no. 754. ISBN-13: 978 0 74781 252 4

Tara Cox has asserted her right under the Copyright, Designs and Patents Act, 1988, to be identified as the author of this book.

Designed by Ken Vail Graphic Design, Cambridge, UK and typeset in Perpetua.

Printed in China through Worldprint Ltd.

13 14 15 16 17   10 9 8 7 6 5 4 3 2 1

COVER IMAGE
Airstreams at a rally. (Wayne Eastep/Getty Images)

TITLE PAGE IMAGE
Airstream trailers have endured for reasons including innovation and durability, but American icon status comes from their magic of capturing the evolving American dream within that perfect tin-can package.

CONTENTS PAGE IMAGE
Not only did Wally Byam manufacture trailers and inspire and deliver a dream to the public, he also offered tidbits on how to make the world a better place. From expecting Airstreamers to always leave a campsite cleaner than it was when they found it to reminding folks to stay calm when trying to communicate in a foreign land, Byam had a simple approach to work, life and traveling that truly contributed to a better world.

ACKNOWLEDGEMENTS
Thank you Robert.

PHOTOGRAPH ACKNOWLEDGEMENTS
Thank you to all who have contributed photographs. Images reproduced courtesy of: Airstream, Inc., pages 3, 4, 7, 10–11, 12, 21, 24, 25 (bottom), 26, 27, 32 (bottom), 33, 35, 36, 37 (bottom), 38, 40 (top), 42, 43, 44, 45, 47; BelRepayre Airstream and Retro Trailer Park, page 57 (bottom); Rory Campbell, page 48; Brad Cornelius, page 52 (bottom); Jacob Davies, page 25 (top); Glen Des Jardins, page 13 (right); Erik Dunham, page 19; Leah Gilberson, page 51; The Grand Daddy Hotel, page 55; Kate's Lazy Desert, pages 56, 57 (top); Sam Keam, page 54 (bottom); Bob Kehoe, page 32 (top); John Long, photographer and Vince Martinico, owner, page 20; Paul Loughridge, page 53 (top); GetFlocked.com, page 46; Susan Measures, pages 18, 54 (top); Mecum Auctions, page 50 (bottom); Brad Mitchell, page 1; Jeremy Noble, page 50 (top); Lee Peters, page 61 (top); Popular Mechanics Magazine, page 8; Mario Ramierz, page 17 (bottom); Tomás N. Romero, page 53 (bottom); Izzy Schwartz, page 52 (top); The Shady Dell, page 55; Steven R. Shook, page 17 (top); Jason C. Smeed, page 61 (bottom); Straight Line Designs, page 60 (bottom); Tin Can Tourists, pages 9, 16 (top), 34; Track 16 Gallery, Santa Monica, CA, page 59; Vroomers.com, page 60 (top); WBCCI, pages 14, 28, 30, 31, 37, 40 (bottom); Dee E. Warenycia, pages 16 (bottom), 22, 23, 62.

Shire Publications is supporting the Woodland Trust, the UK's leading woodland conservation charity, by funding the dedication of trees.

CONTENTS

THE MAN

A CREATION as iconic as an Airstream trailer certainly couldn't have come from an ordinary man. The company's creator, Wallace Merle Byam, was born on July 4, 1896, and it took him years to realize the excitement surrounding his birthday wasn't for him. Part adventurer, part showman, Byam was an innovator, entrepreneur, sharp businessman and public relations genius who kept up the hoopla throughout his life. He not only created an everlasting icon but also maintained a successful business, led hundreds on worldwide expeditions and acted as an ambassador for the average American throughout the world.

Abandoned by his father, Byam and his mother lived with various relatives during his youth. At the age of twelve he was put in charge of a flock of sheep for the summer. Alone with the animals in the outdoors, he lived in a canvas-topped two-wheeled vehicle pulled by a donkey. The tailboard came down, and behind it was a sleeping mat, a small stove and some space for food, water, a wash pail and some books. Though it couldn't take him far or fast, this was Byam's first experience with a moveable home and it certainly became a reference point when designing trailers.

Not long after he graduated from high school, Wally's mother and stepfather died within two weeks of each other. Reflecting on life, Wally compiled a list of goals for himself:

1. Cease this easy-go-lucky stuff
2. Cultivate a memory
3. Get enjoyment out of little things
4. Cultivate willpower
5. Don't live for past or future. Make history.

Just before he left Stanford University, Byam paused for more self-reflection and goal-setting. He was twenty-one when he wrote, "I am a man of

In the mid-twentieth century, Wally Byam's adventurous spirit shrunk the world down into the palm of his hand. Airstreams famously visited landmarks such as The Leaning Tower of Pisa, the Great Pyramids of Egypt, L'Arc de Triomphe and Chichen Itza. In 1963 they literally drove around the globe in the 31,000-mile, 403-day Around the World Caravan.

extremes—either I will be a big boss, a rousing success, or a blank failure. In my heart I know I'll be a great big glorious success, and that my name will go down in history."

Upon graduating from Stanford with a law degree in the early 1920s Byam took jobs in advertising copywriting, worked as the national advertising manager of a newspaper and spent his early career on the advertising side of start-up magazines. He later formed his own agency, publishing do-it-yourself magazines, which were quite popular at the time. This varied knowledge of running businesses, communications, marketing and public relations would come in handy later when Byam promoted his trailers.

On June 24, 1924, Byam married Marion E. James, a woman not exactly known for her love of sleeping on the ground. As legend has it, she stated she would not go camping without her kitchen … so Byam complied by developing and perfecting a travel trailer.

While working on his own magazine in the late 1920s, he bought an article on how to build a travel trailer, a hobby that was gaining popularity at the time. Unfortunately, the plans brought in complaints from readers about how they didn't work, which inspired Byam to build the trailer from the plans himself. Seeing the flaws, Wally proceeded to develop new plans to instruct people on how to *properly* build a trailer in your own backyard— and for not a lot of money.

In developing the perfect trailer, Byam faced a few challenges: his wife's needs; the flaws of the original design; and his own vision. An early Byam trailer consisted of a box on a Model T chassis. Once parked, a tent could be erected on the platform, keeping the sleepers off the ground. A small shelf held a water bottle, flashlight and some other very basic equipment, keeping them and the campers protected from the elements. Yet, this didn't satisfy Marion, who didn't like the "rough" aspects of sleeping in a tent. In addition, one had to crawl into it, which made getting dressed extremely difficult. This inspired Byam to innovate, so he created a set of moveable drawers, which could be pulled to the ground. The tent could then be set up on top of the drawers, raising the height of the tent and making dressing while standing up possible.

His plans still evolving, Byam moved on to develop a wooden teardrop-shaped trailer on a platform with an enclosed ice chest, and a kerosene stove. Always testing his own creations, a camping trip in this rig garnered the Byams so much attention, questions and requests that Wally concluded this could end up being a good business plan.

There is some haze around the exact origins of Byam's own first published plans. Byam stated he published an article in *Popular Mechanics* magazine entitled "How to Build a Trailer for One Hundred Dollars," but no such article can be located. Perhaps it was published in one of the many

WORLD TRAVELING LAND LINER

MADRID   BRUXELLES   ROME   PARIS   *LONDON   BERLIN
BARCELONA   LIEGE   MILANO   VERSAILLES   .IVERPOOL   HAMBURG
SEVILLE   BASTOGNE   VENEZIA   BREST   .LLANDUDNO   COLOGNE
MALAGA   LUXEMBOURG   FLORENCE   OSTEND   EDINBURGH   BONN
GRANADA   HELSINKI   NAPLES   LYON   >WLHELI   FRANKFURT
BURGOS   DUNKIRK   GENOA   MARSAILLES   OURNEMOUTH   HEIDELBERG
SAN SEBASTIAN CHATEAU THIERRY ALASSIO NICE   >OVER   MUNCH
                                       MONTE CARLO   XFORD   STUTTGART

"popular" hobby magazines of the times or perhaps Wally printed an article in one of his own do-it-yourself magazines. The most likely scenario is that he took out an ad for plans to build your own trailer. He sold them for $1 a piece and proceeded to make $15,000 as the requests rolled in.

Around this time, a neighbor asked Byam if he would make a trailer for him. Byam began producing made-to-order trailers out of his backyard, often inviting the customer over to pitch in if they wanted (to this day, customers are always invited to stop by the Airstream factory to see how things are coming along). The backyard business eventually became a nuisance to the neighbors and a little more than Byam could handle, so a change was in order.

Byam shifted operations and opened a small trailer factory in Culver City, California, in 1931. From the start of production he began to put into practice the "let's not make changes, only improvements" philosophy he was later known for. These included lowering the floor so one could stand inside, and incorporating the ice chest and a kerosene stove he used in his own early trailer along with a bed. In 1932 the first "Airstreams" were for sale, named so because they traveled like a "stream of air." It is to be noted that the debut model—the 1932 Torpedo Car Cruiser—was still made of plywood; the next two models, though named the "Silver Bullet" and "Silver Cloud," were also made of Masonite (a type of hardboard made of pressed-wood fibers); the iconic silver bullet look was still a little way in the future.

In 1952 Wally Byam and trailering pal Cornelius Vanderbilt Jr. traveled on a factory-finding/PR mission in a specially built trailer called the "Commodore." This Airstream also served as a mobile cocktail lounge. Note the names of places visited painted on the trailer, something Byam did on his well-traveled trailers.

7

A 1930s article from *Popular Mechanics* magazine illustrates both the popularity of trailering and streamlining. A grandfather builds a streamlined trailer for his granddaughters that they can pull with their streamlined tricycle.

"Tourist" Trailer for Youngsters Is Towed by a Tricycle

Touring the seashore at Venice, Calif., is a streamline trailer towed by a streamline tricycle. Tiny as it is, the miniature trailer is big enough for two little girls to "keep house" in as they play on the beach. Their grandfather built the two-wheel trailer.

Two sisters tour a California beach with a tricycle and a miniature trailer built by their grandfather

When the young Wally contemplated where to go in life, he said:

I just hate the idea of being a business man or running a big mill or anything like that. I do not know whether to make myself like that kind of life or become a beachcomber, as in the play. One way gives me success, renown and prestige and the other gives me happiness. Which shall I choose?

Though he probably didn't know it in 1931, but with the birth of Airstream, Byam would not have to choose. He ended up being both the businessman *and* the beachcomber.

Starting a trailer business of this type in the early 1930s ended up being very good timing. The onset of the Great Depression actually fueled sales of Airstream (and trailers in general). As people were forced to go on the move to seek out sources of income, homes on wheels became a good investment for following the work. The industry boomed: in 1932 there were forty-eight trailer companies but within five years there were over four hundred.

In the mid- to late 1930s, Byam placed classified ads in *Popular Mechanics* magazine selling do-it-yourself plans and blueprints for building your own Airstream trailer. It is said that an early ad similar to this earned Byam $15,000.

BUILD THE "AIRSTREAM" TRAILER

MODERN, light, strong. Actually built *within* bridge construction side walls, eliminating old-fashioned platform frame. Length 13 ft. Four big beds, shower, toilet, ship's galley, refrig., clothes closet. Easy to build at home, no machine tools needed. Materials cost $150. Complete building instructions, photos, $1.00. Detailed Blue Prints $5.00.
BYAM PRESS   134 So. St. Andrews Place   LOS ANGELES, CAL.

All this was even before Airstream's iconic design came about. Though a savvy businessman and dedicated tinkerer and improver, Byam didn't actually come up with the now-familiar design. The original aluminum trailer was actually designed by William Hawley Bowlus in 1934. With a background in airplane design (he was part of the team who built Charles Lindbergh's "Spirit of St. Louis"), Bowlus built his trailer in the spirit of the airplanes of the time—riveted aluminum that was lightweight and easy to tow. More of a designer and less of a businessman, the Bowlus-Teller Trailer Company went under in 1936 and Byam scooped up what was left. After some minor modifications Byam's first aluminum trailer debuted in 1936, named the Airstream Clipper, and sold for $1,200.

The Clipper contained a kerosene stove, water was carried in cans and toilets were not invented yet. "Nothing good enough has been invented," stated Byam at the time. Travelers used a chamber pot or "thunder mug," which was emptied where sanitary and convenient.

No sooner was an icon born than the industry started to decline. By 1937 Airstream began to have financial problems and Byam moved operations twice to cut costs. The onset of World War II only made things worse, as aluminum was classified as a critical war material and eventually the War Production Board ordered the suspension of the production of travel trailers for personal use. In 1942, Byam closed the plant and found work in the aviation industry.

The 1936 Airstream Clipper was Byam's first riveted aluminum trailer. Inspired by Hawley Bowlus's Road Chief, it was Airstream's first "Silver Bullet" by design.

According to Byam, trailering provides one with the following "Four Freedoms": The freedom from arrangements (no worries about reservations or schedules), the freedom from problems of age (travel eliminates boredom and therefore keeps people young), the freedom to know ("a tourist can never see a country the way a trailerite does") and the freedom for fun (the other freedoms allow time and energy for this one!).

After the war, Byam wanted to get back to trailer making, but finances made it difficult. A man named Curtis Wright capitalized on the similarity of his name to the aviation company Curtiss-Wright Industries (of Wright Brothers fame) and began building trailers after the war. Byam entered into an agreement with Wright and introduced the Curtis Wright Clipper, which was essentially the Airstream Clipper. This arrangement did not last long. Byam needed to be his own boss, so once he was back on his feet, Wallace Manufacturing was founded, and eventually replaced with the the launch of Airstream Trailers, Inc. on November 1, 1948.

Relaunching was difficult after the war as the company had no cash reserves, just Byam's perseverance and his dedicated employees. He was an inspiring leader—he was not afraid to speak his mind and he wouldn't take no for an answer. It was said he had an unusual way of giving confidence to his employees—he simply stated they could do it and they not only believed it, they did it. This sort of dedication is demonstrated by the tales of employees pitching in from their own pockets to help purchase a part for a trailer so Byam could make the sale.

With Byam's wartime knowledge of the aviation industry under his belt, the Airstream Liner was released in 1947 as an all-aluminum trailer and pretty soon the company went on to release seven liners, all named for a different type of wind: Southwind Breeze, Chinook, Tradewind, Westwind, Zephyr and SeaBreeze.

During this postwar period trailers hit a bit of a speed bump as well. Though demand for them grew, the industry expanded in a way that Byam felt was wrong. The travel trailer was evolving from something that one used to get up and go into more of a stationary item. The need for housing for newly married GIs led people to live in trailers, which were a cheaper alternative to houses because builders could get around housing codes. As this need for cheap housing increased, permanent sites for trailers began to appear, which was completely contrary to Byam's philosophy. According to Byam, trailers were a "go-places thing." He resented these stationary trailers even being called trailers as he wanted his product to reflect not only being on the move but honesty, quality and integrity in the product itself, which these new structures often lacked. "These trailers built for permanent occupancy in fixed locations have their own sponsors. I am not one of them," stated Byam.

Along with these permanent trailer homes came a cultural distaste for trailer folk and new regulations that inhibited the freedom of the original traveling trailerites. Eventually the new homes were distinguished as "mobile homes" but the reputation of the true trailerite was forever tarnished.

As Byam's business expanded, he did not preside over his company from behind a desk; he was also an active user of his own Airstream. After his marriage to Marion ended, Wally met his second wife Estelle "Stella" North Hall on a trailer trip. Stella was known as a fun-loving, free-spirited gal who loved the outdoors. They were married on September 5, 1953.

Wally Byam hanging out at the Airstream factory as his wife Stella brings him a soda. He once said, "Just as all the world loves a lover, in my experience all the world loves a trailerite."

Byam was a man who could not sit still and wasn't happy unless he was innovating, exploring and learning; he truly enjoyed the fruits of his labors. He loved the challenge of building a trailer, he loved the trailering lifestyle and once on the road he would take note of issues, problems and weaknesses in his product so he could assess them and bring improvements back to the factory.

Always one to build upon what he was already doing, routine trips led to group trips. At one point, Byam thought it would be fun to put a group together to explore Central America and so the first Wally Byam Caravan was born. After many trials and tribulations, the trip was ultimately a success, bringing to light the spirit, camaraderie and determination of Airstreamers. With this trip Byam also had the added bonus of seeing his creation perform in more difficult circumstances, leading him to even more improvements in the durability of the trailer. This caravan also served as a fantastic (and fun) form of public relations for the company; if you introduce people to the dream, they will want to buy your product to achieve their own.

This initial caravan led to many more in Wally's lifetime and the creation of the Wally Byam Caravan Club International (WBCCI). Caravanners traveled to Europe, Central America, Africa and eventually around the world. Until the end of his life, the caravans served as an important part of the company's image and were where Byam devoted most of his time and energy. Gaining much attention wherever they went (and back home as well), Byam felt the caravanners served as American ambassadors of the "regular people" and did more good for international relations than official visits from dignitaries.

His respect for foreign lands and people is clearly shown by the advice he gave trailerites: "If you really want to get to know a country, go traveling through it." He had much wisdom when it came to traveling and international relations with gems such as,

> When you first find yourself in a foreign country where you can't understand anybody and nobody can understand you … your first inclination is to keep repeating over and over again. Your next feeling is to shout. They hear you all right. They just don't understand you. You are the dumb foreigner. Not they.

Byam wrote two books during the caravan heyday, *Fifth Avenue on Wheels* (1953) followed by *Trailer Travel Here and Abroad* (1960). Both were accounts of the trailer life, with *Fifth Avenue* focusing on how to get started trailering, offering tips about the lifestyle, and *Trailer Travel* focusing more on the exotic travels of Byam and the caravans. Both books are wonderful representations of Byam in his own words. They express the love he had for trailers, his company and traveling in a tin can on wheels. His zest for life shows through with his good humor, open perspective and hard work.

In 1962 Byam died of a brain tumor. His spirit lives on through the trailers—between 60 and 70 percent of all Airstreams built are still on the road today—the Caravan Club, Airstream owners, innovators and fans. Airstream is the only remaining trailer company left from the height of trailering in the mid-twentieth century. Icon, indeed.

Below right: Byam's first book, *Fifth Avenue on Wheels* (1953), starts out giving readers practical instruction and tips on buying and outfitting a trailer and goes on to fan the dreams of wanderlust as he shares tales of his world travels, all the while proving the thesis of his title.

Below left: Byam's second book, *Trailer Travel Here and Abroad* (1960), reads as an entertaining manual for caravanning around the world. Modestly boastful and inspirational, Byam shares the challenges he and his fellow travelers faced and overcame, making around-the-world adventures seem within reach.

1935

AIRSTREAM
1935 TORPEDO
THE OLDEST EXISTING
AIRSTREAM TRAILER IN THE WORLD

THE TRAILER

"Let's not make changes, let's make only improvements."

Wally Byam

THE EARLIEST AIRSTREAMS were wood-framed and Masonite-skinned; they were absolutely not silver or bullet-like. Teardrop-shaped and with a wood or leather cloth exterior, they were an improvement on what was already out there but not yet as durable, sturdy or good-looking as they would become. Quality and innovation were always important to Byam, who felt that a well-built trailer was its own best salesman.

In Airstream's case, function bred form and eventually led to a spectacular look. According to Byam the precursor to the travel trailer was not the covered wagon as so many say, but the trunk and luggage rack of the old Model T. It wasn't uncommon to see camping equipment strapped to the roof and front and back bumpers of the old cars with passengers taking to the road for fun and adventure.

After discovering that the building plans for a travel trailer published in his magazine were inadequate, Byams was inspired to tinker with trailers in order to improve the design. His improvements were shaped by his experience of sleeping in a cart as a teenager, and his wife's requirements. Kinks in his designs were worked out on trailer trips, innovation by the competition led to a design overhaul, and finally input from customers and travels around the world led to bigger and better improvements.

Airstream's first model, the Torpedo Car Cruiser, was the result of building upon an existing plan—constantly tinkering and improving. The first big innovation was the lowering of the floor, giving the occupants more headroom and, as a result, comfort.

Recreational Vehicles (RVs) are often compared to boats (they're even referred to as land yachts); however, Byam wrote that they were actually unable to adopt a single design feature from boats for the trailers. Boats are not designed for comfort, and are limited by the shape of the hull. In contrast, Airstreams were all about the occupants' experience and comfort.

Opposite:
In 1984 Airstream, Inc. officially recognized this 1935 Airstream Torpedo as the oldest existing Airstream. It took two years for Dr. Norman Holman to built it from a set of plans in *Popular Mechanics* magazine.

Right: Dr. Norman Holman and his wife Thelma in front of the 1935 Airstream Torpedo he built. It took its first trip in 1937 and still makes the rounds of rallies and gatherings proudly displaying its title as the oldest existing Airstream.

Below: "The aerodynamic shape is functional in such a beautiful, simple way. Instead of showing the hand of the designer through ornamentation, the design gets its power through the ruthless elimination of any sort of ornament—it is pure function," wrote James Meigs, editor-in-chief, *Popular Mechanics*.

Byam pointed out in *Fifth Avenue on Wheels*: "Nobody was more flabbergasted than the trailer manufacturers themselves when they found people coming home from their vacations and continuing to live in their trailers in preference to their own homes. Life was simpler, easier. They liked it."

The biggest "improvement" in the Airstream trailer was the introduction of the riveted aluminum trailer. Though Byam cannot be credited with this invention, he certainly can be credited with improving on a sharp design and turning it into an everlasting icon.

By the 1930s, "streamlining" was becoming a trend as it was realised that form and function could coexist to improve one another. From airplanes

to cars, design was becoming influenced by performance. This new look, a branch of the popular Art Deco movement, was dubbed "Streamline Moderne." A shiny silver color, and lines that suggested forward movement and speed both contributed to this futuristic look. Originally, the design *did* help performance in moving vehicles, such as trains, but it was the suggestion of movement in stationary objects that stuck as a trend. Pretty soon this design was being applied to everything from typewriters to toasters; these unsexy objects suddenly had a look that suggested passion, speed, faith in American design and moving forward into the future. One of the best

Electrical Products Building

New York World's Fair 1939   A-30

A postcard from the 1939 World's Fair in New York is another example of the stark, strong stylings of Streamline Moderne. The look was futuristic, hopeful and thoroughly modern.

The Streamline Moderne style was essentially Art Deco stripped of its embellishments (streamlined). This detail on a modern diner building clearly shows the rounded edges and clean lines of this art movement.

examples of this design was the look of the 1939 World's Fair. Fritz Lang's film *Metropolis* also incorporates this look.

The Bowlus Road Chief was the first riveted aluminum trailer and the first trailer to fall under the Streamline Moderne look. Bowlus modeled his trailer after the light-bodied aircrafts of the time. Riveted aluminum panels were attached to welded steel tubing, resulting in an extremely lightweight body. The aluminum was actually a material called Duralumin—an alloy of aluminum, copper, and magnesium. It was as strong as steel, but one-third of the weight. Bowlus started tinkering in 1933, and by 1934 his trailer was ready. Besides the lightweight aluminum body, Bowlus' 1934 Road Chief was the first with a door within a door, located above the hitch. This model allowed for a porch platform before entering in the trailer and also allowed airflow while the main door was closed. This trailer was more expensive, and geared towards luxury.

Legend is fuzzy about how Wally originally became involved with the Bowlus Trailer Company; some say he moonlighted at a dealership that sold Bowlus trailers or perhaps he sold them from his own trailer lot. The Bowlus Trailer Company hit hard times in 1935 and took on an investor, Jacob Teller. After a few months, Teller pulled out of the Bowlus-Teller Trailer Company

The Bowlus Road Chief closely resembled the fuselage of an airplane of the time. With its bullet shape and clean lines, it is clearly an example of Streamline Moderne design. Today original Bowlus trailers are extremely rare as only about eighty were built during the company's existence.

and after other unsuccessful investor relationships the company had to close its doors in 1935, and Bowlus went back to airplane manufacturing. Byam, ever the savvy businessman, purchased much of the equipment from the bankrupt company and introduced *his* first aluminum travel trailer, the Airstream Clipper. The main differences between the Road Chief and the Clipper include the number of panels, frame configurations, the location of the door (Byam moved it from behind the hitch to the side of the trailer), and the window-opening mechanism. Among other improvements Byam added water pumps and gas stoves. On January 17, 1936, the Airstream Clipper (named in honor of the Pan Am Clipper airplanes) was the first semi-monocoque (construction found in planes where the outer shell supports most of the weight) trailer under the Airstream brand. The semi-monocoque construction provided higher strength with less weight, the aerodynamic shape required less horsepower to pull (improving gas mileage) and it provided smoother towing. The Airstream had electric lights, slept four, carried its own water supply and had a dry-ice air-conditioning system. At $1,200 it was expensive, but demand was high despite the Depression. The two trailer manufacturers both put out a 1936 model, with Bowlus building about eighty trailers during his company's production run, while Byam sold

The Airstream Clipper, Byam's first riveted aluminum trailer, was inspired by Bowlus's Road Chief but still had a distinctive look of its own. Some say it resembles an alien or a medieval helmet.

Both the Bowlus Road Chief (foreground) and the Airstream Clipper had 1936 models. Byam's main changes were the tail-end windows resembling alien eyes and moving the door from the hitch to the side.

the Clipper to order, producing about thirty to forty prewar aluminum Airstream trailers. With the introduction of the Clipper, an icon was born. According to James Meigs, editor-in-chief of *Popular Mechanics* magazine:

> This is an elegantly simple object, totally optimized for one thing: slipping through the air. You'd think that clean perfection would be marred somewhat by the visible seams and rivets, but it is just the opposite. That little bit of texture shows you that this is essentially a hand-made object, like an airplane. And instead of hiding that workmanship behind some veneer, the Airstream shows it off proudly. It reveals its engineering, like a DC-3 or a Mercury capsule.

Over his lifetime Byam kept innovating by listening to customer feedback and taking trips in his own trailers to further his quest to develop a truly self-contained trailer. Integrity was (and still is) a huge part of the fabric of the company. Byam stood behind its product and offered this lifetime guarantee: "Anything that goes wrong that could possibly be our fault will be repaired without charge at the factory for as long as you own your Airstream." Byam's goal was self-containment, which represented true independence because external hookups and power sources were not needed. He once said he wanted to build a trailer that "my lovely old grandmother might tow … to the middle of the Gobi Desert, there to live in gracious metropolitan luxury … without reloading, refueling, recharging or regretting." He strove for the best, inspiring others to develop new gadgets for his trailer. Over the years, innovations such as the Byam Burner (a compact heating system), the Dometic refrigerator (a fridge that didn't need ice to stay cold), the first workable hot-water system for a trailer, and the first flushable toilet, set Airstream apart. Airstream was the first fully self-contained travel trailer making Byam's dream come true in 1957 with the Airstream International. Trailerites were dreamers: they wanted to add this, improve that, so they ate up the company's gadgets and improvements. Pretty soon trailers were competing with homes!

It has been said that Byam constantly threw challenges out at his staff and had a way of inspiring and pushing his employees to accomplish what had been previously thought to be impossible. Here, a blue-beret wearing Byam (front row, fifth from right) visits an Airstream plant.

Byam looked down on mobile homes, along with the shoddy construction that was associated with them. As trailer parks filled with mobile homes began to develop, Byam felt that trailering began to get a "black eye" and he was happy when differentiation was made. But as for true trailering in general, Byam felt, "For ease and comfort, lack of work and genuine luxury, you can't beat trailering. It is truly and honestly Fifth Avenue on wheels."

Before World War II, Byam had established a reputable company, a strong look and a solid product. Postwar, Airstream took on even more new life. Many factors drive something to iconic status—integrity, durability, a look, the lifestyle, enduring advertising, a tight-knit community—Airstream had all of these. The passion goes beyond the trailer itself, but is ingrained in the fantasy that Airstream advertising and marketing created, promoted and celebrated.

After World War II, Airstream focused on strengthening the product itself and developing the dream even further. Trailer caravans were testing grounds for improvement and durability. As the trips got more ambitious and the terrain more difficult, Byam took note of the trailers' performance—both his own and those of his fellow caravanners—and made the necessary adjustments. Byam certainly spent his time making improvements, not changes. In 1957 the trailer became self-contained with the International model, and in 1961 the Bambi was introduced—the first small self-contained travel trailer.

The Argosy, also known as "The Painted Airstream," served as a testing ground for new features before they were incorporated into the Airstream. The front wrap window is one example.

In December 1967 Airstream was purchased by Beatrice Foods, a company whose very name suggests that trailers were not their specialty. Some say the Beatrice years were dark years, when Byam's level of integrity was compromised. The early days started out well, with a 1969 redesign that introduced a longer, wider and overall rounder shape. As time went on smaller trailers were discontinued and the Class A motorhome was introduced. True to the 1970s aesthetic of covering up what was formerly—and would once again be—considered beautiful, the company introduced vinyl-covered cabinets, shag carpeting and dark wood-grain interiors. Structural changes included reducing the frame size, moving the bathroom to the rear and introducing the grey-water tank. As the interiors became heavier, sagging frames became a problem.

In 1972 Airstream introduced the Argosy trailer. Known now as the painted Airstream, it was a test ground for new features, which if successful were incorporated into other models. Though many thought it was a traditional riveted aluminum Airstream with a paint job, it was actually produced differently, being made up of one piece of steel, not five aluminum segments as in traditional Airstream models.

The boxy shape of the Airstream Land Yacht trailer earned it the nickname "Squarestream." Airstream purists were offended by this mutation of their beloved design and Squarestreams were initially not allowed into the WBCCI.

In 1974 the company launched its first motorhome, also under the Argosy name. In 1979 the Airstream Classic motorhome was launched—a silver recreational vehicle (RV) that was more reminiscent of the traditional Airstream look. That same year, Airstream lost $12 million dollars due to gas shortages, high financing rates and less demand for recreational vehicles in general. The RV industry was in a depression.

Luckily, in July 1979, Beatrice sold the company to Thor Industries. Thor was a start-up RV company, and Airstream was its first acquisition. The general perception is that Thor brought integrity back to the company; they went on to innovate in a style more in line with Byam's. In 1986 Thor reintroduced the Argosy with different lines, and by 1988 and 1989 a fifth-wheel (a larger travel trailer with a special hitch mounted over the rear axle of a pickup truck) and a motorhome respectively were introduced, both called the Airstream Land Yacht. In order to compete with the popular squared-off RVs of the time, the company abandoned the traditional Airstream silhouette for these models in favor of the trend. Airstream enthusiasts were not amused and dubbed the fifth-wheel the "Squarestream." Sales were not good. Even the Wally Byam Caravan Club refused it admission into the club (though they've since changed the rules).

In the 1990s all Airstreams became widebodies, with 6 inches added to the width; this was the first major redesign since 1969. The Safari was

Below left and opposite bottom: In the early 2000s, architect Christopher Deam's modern minimalist interiors helped steer the company in a new direction. With Deam's designs, the interiors were now as cool as the exteriors, appealing to a younger demographic.

introduced as a more affordable model and was popular among first-time Airstream customers.

By the 2000s, as the trailer became more popular with successful young people, the company introduced interiors designed by noted San Francisco architect Christopher Deam. Deam created minimalistic, modern interiors that matched the gorgeous exterior of the trailer.

In the early twenty-first century Airstream branched out to create other variations on the icon. The Ford Airstream was a futuristic concept car/sports utility vehicle debuted in 2007 as a partnership between Airstream and Ford. The exterior gave a nod towards the classic Airstream look but with a modern future-retro spin. The interior—which included a 360-degree screen for entertainment and games, including ambient mood settings like

Above:
The Airstream Land Yacht Class A motorhome was an instant success, outselling the company's first Class A motorhome, the Classic. Though still falling under the Squarestream label, this design seemed to be more palatable in a motorhome.

Above: The Ford Airstream concept car debuted in 2007 as a futuristic plug-in hybrid. Inspired by the film *2001: A Space Odyssey*, it was meant to feel like a loungey spaceship for the ultimate in travel comfort.

In the early 2000s, Airstream collaborated with Chevrolet and Mercedes-Benz on Class B motorhomes. The Chevrolet Avenue and the Mercedes-Benz Interstate (pictured) offer alternatives to a traditional motorhome or trailer.

a lava lamp and fireplace. This, and the fact that it was a plug-in hybrid hydrogen fuel cell, made it all-modern. The Nissan Base Camp was a tiny ultra-light tent trailer almost reminiscent of the very first Airstreams but with a modern futuristic appeal. Two Class B motorhomes, Airstream Avenue (a collaboration with Chevrolet) and the Airstream Interstate (a collaboration with Mercedes-Benz), were part of the company's range in the early twenty-first century.

Though there have been other iterations, changes, trends and collaborations, it's the semi-monocoque aluminum trailer that remains the most beloved Airstream design. And though it has adapted to the times, been improved and modernized, its essence hasn't really changed much from that original 1936 Clipper, and it is the sole survivor of its peers of the nearly four hundred trailer companies of the late 1930s (though in 2013, the Bowlus Road Chief was reintroduced in the United States).

Airstream's Jackson Center, Ohio plant offers factory tours to the public. This is a holdover from the days when Byam welcomed customers into his backyard to watch or help as he assembled their trailers.

THE COMMUNITY

"Whether we like it or not, any fool can see this earth is gradually becoming one world."

Wally Byam

RVers are known to be a friendly bunch, and Airstreamers are no exception. In fact, through the efforts of Wally Byam, Airstream owners might just be the most friendly goodwill ambassadors not only within North America, but also across the world!

The communities that have been formed around the common bond of Airstreams are similar to any other enthusiast clubs, such as those for classic cars or Harley-Davidsons. With an Airstream, however, the vehicle doesn't just go from place to place, it's your actual home in that place. As a result the sense of community gets extended past the point of a head nod or a wave to a neighborly bond. Throw in some minor travel hardships to solve together and you've practically got yourself a family. Though many groups exist, the main and most impressive is the Wally Byam Caravan Club International (WBCCI).

Always practicing what he preached, Byam was an avid and adventurous trailerite. In 1951 he noticed that a customer didn't seem to be enjoying his trailer as much as he could, so Byam invited him on a trip to southern California to show him the ropes. Things went so well they discussed taking their trailers further than ever before—all the way to Central America. After inviting a few more people, word got out and suddenly fifty trailers signed up for the adventure. On the day they were scheduled to leave, December 1, 1951, sixty-three trailers showed up ready to hit the road.

Byam was a natural leader and organized as much as possible before the trip. Generators, advance arrangements for parking, camping supplies, border crossings etc—he thought of almost everything. He proposed that all caravanners pay a blanket charge so that they would have cash on hand for group expenses. With this he also purchased towing equipment, spare

Opposite:
An aerial shot of a camp in Monterey, Mexico, 1955 shows the circular parking pattern of the trailers. Meetings and other gatherings were held in the center of the circle.

A happy WBCCI couple in front of a vintage trailer. The man sports the club's signature blue beret. Many other traditions started by Byam's early caravans are continued today, such as labeling the trailers with the owners' membership numbers in red.

parts and organized guides and police to travel with what would be the first trailer caravan in history.

Byam handed out blue berets to those who joined the caravan, both for fun and for identification. He had begun wearing his signature cap in 1948 while in Europe and bought extra to give as gifts to friends and customers: "I found that the beret made a wonderful trailer headgear. It kept your head warm, kept your hair in place, and gave you some protection when popping in and out of low doors. Best of all, you could roll it up and put it in your pocket." Caravanners got a kick out of it and the wearing of the beret stuck. It was adopted as an official symbol when the club became organized in 1955.

Excitement was high, but the trip was tough. By the time they got to the halfway point at Mexico City, almost a third had given up and gone home. Byam reminded those remaining that the trip would get even more difficult, including a treacherous train ride through the jungle in which the trailers would be piggy-backed to the train cars. The die-hards continued south to Guatemala, and on to El Salvador, Honduras and Nicaragua, encountering myriad problems along the way. Byam always stayed positive, even if he wasn't sure what was ahead. After a bout of Byam's optimism upon encountering a particularly rocky, holey, rugged road, the group good-naturedly dubbed it a Byam Boulevard. Byam cannibalized his own trailer to repair other trailers so much he abandoned it on the side of the road. The trip lasted three months and fourteen trailers out of the original sixty-three endured the return trip to the US.

After all they had been through on the three-month trip, Byam vowed never to do it again; until he realized that despite all the hardships they sustained, he and the other participants ended up talking about the wonderful time they had had on the trip. Nine months later, in November 1952, taking what he learned from the first trip, Byam organized another caravan to Mexico.

Certain protocols for trailer caravans were established during the first two trips that would be developed, perfected and maintained over time. The first caravan established some early organizational features that continue until this day, including a number assigned to and painted on each trailer so they could be checked in at each stop. Names were also painted on the trailers to make it easier to find each other in camp.

After a few trips, the caravan club was running like a true democracy. Caravans were made up of people from all walks of life—bankers, teachers, farmers, and doctors—and all contributed their expertise in one way or another. On the first night of the first caravan, the trailers parked in a circle, as it was easier to unhitch the cars that way. It also allowed for a more democratic set-up in which everyone was equal. As the caravans expanded, concentric circles became the model, with festivities, meetings and group activities taking place in the center of the circle which everyone could easily access. According to Byam, "A circle is a pretty democratic thing; nobody on any part of the perimeter has an advantage over anybody else."

Below left: Helen Byam Schwamborn, Byam's cousin and WBCCI member number two, served as the first editor of the club newsletter. The first issue was published in July 1964.

Below right: Over fifty years later, WBCCI members receive a subscription to Blue Beret magazine, filling them in on all sorts of club-related information. Non-WBCCI members and all Airstream enthusiasts can read all about their favorite trailer lifestyle in Airstream Life magazine.

Right:
Wally and Stella's gold Airstream built especially for the African Caravan. Byam abandoned an idea of coloring trailers in Easter-egg colors to match the color schemes of 1950s automobiles when he realized from his own trailer that anodizing didn't produce an even color.

Below:
A desert scene from the Capetown to Cairo caravan, complete with mingling Airstreams and camels. Trailerites have stated that no matter where they went with their Airstreams, they were always welcomed warmly.

Other organizational features included meetings, voting to settle all queries, bookkeeping and a kitty for group expenses. Committees were set up to cover the different aspects of life on the road, with the real-world experience of doctors, accountants and so on carried over to the group. The caboose was a mechanic who followed the group to make sure no one was left behind. A true team effort, one of the main things caravanners learned from the experience was how to cooperate under pressure.

The third trip was planned for eastern Canada in 1954. Because Byam was off scouting for a caravan to Europe, he put his cousin Helen Byam Schwamborn (who had never towed a trailer!) in charge. During this trip the caravanners decided to formalize the group, and the official Wally Byam Caravan Club

International, Inc. (WBCCI) was founded on August 3, 1955 in Kentville, Nova Scotia. There were thirty-nine charter members. Helen served as the first editor of the club newsletter, *The Blue Beret*, named for Byam's signature cap. The newsletter became a magazine in July 1964.

Byam was a sensitive traveler and wanted to represent Americans in the best light possible. He reminded his trailerites:

> Many American tourists have a tendency to suppose that our habits and customs are correct and superior to all others, that our high standard of living gives us this prerogative. But does it really? ... Precisely because we do have opportunities and advantages others cannot afford, Americans should be especially understanding abroad.

When a caravan rolled into town, it was certainly a big deal. They were received by mayors, governors, civic organizations and even presidents. According to Byam, "We feel that we have spread more honest-to-goodness, down to earth goodwill in the countries we've visited than all the striped-pants diplomats put together."

There were two-dozen caravans from the first until Wally's death in 1962. Each one was larger and more ambitious than the last, from touring Europe in 1956 to the famous 1959 Capetown to Cairo trip—when the Byams traveled through Africa in a gold-anodized-aluminum Airstream! In 1963 a group even took a trip around the world, though sadly this was after Byam's passing.

In the 1960s, the company's brilliant marketing included beautiful images of active Airstreamers enjoying their trailers and having adventures around the world. Here WBCCI members pose in front of the bas-relief of Sapor I in Iran.

Membership card for the Tin Can Tourists from 1922. The Tin Can Tourists were founded in 1919 and met up until the 1980s. To become a member of the group, prospective members had to sing the official song, "The More We Get Together." Revived in 1998, the group is open to all makes and models of vintage trailers.

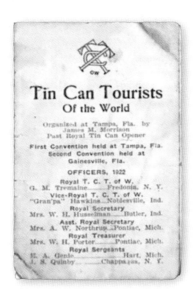

Tin Can Tourists
Of the World

Organized at Tampa, Fla. by
James M. Morrison
Past Royal Tin Can Opener

First Convention held at Tampa, Fla.
Second Convention held at
Gainesville, Fla.

OFFICERS, 1922
Royal T. C. T. of W.
G. M. Tremaine........Fredonia, N. Y.
Vice-Royal T. C. T. of W.
"Gran'pa" Hawkins..Noblesville, Ind.
Royal Secretary
Mrs. W. H. Husselman....Butler, Ind.
Asst. Royal Secretary
Mrs. A. W. Northrup..Pontiac, Mich.
Royal Treasurer
Mrs. W. H. Porter........Pontiac, Mich.
Royal Sergeants
E. A. Genie............Hart, Mich.
J. S. Quinby........Chappaqua, N. Y.

These trips were instrumental in Airstream's marketing. National magazines covered the trips and wowed those back home with images of the familiar trailers in exotic locales. A mini-series narrated by Vincent Price called the *Around the World Caravan* brought the wonder of world trailer travel into people's homes. The word of mouth surrounding Airstream's marketing created a desire in the public to be a part of this community.

In the early twenty-first century WBCCI had more than twelve thousand members and a few intra-clubs for more special-interest Airstreamers. The two most notable are the Vintage Airstream Club and the Classic Airstream Club, two titles that are initially difficult to differentiate, but upon further inspection are quite different. Bud and Bettye Cooper formed the Vintage Airstream Club in 1993 as a group for WBCCI members who own Airstreams more than twenty-five years old. Meanwhile the Classic Airstream club is for members who own Airstreams with the classic silver-bullet look, regardless of age. No motorhomes, squarestreams or Argosys can join the Classic Airstream Club.

Though perhaps the largest, WBCCI isn't the only community that has formed around Airstreams. Sisters on the Fly was founded in 1999 by a group of women who enjoyed camping and being outside together. Though not exclusive to Airstreams, many members are proud owners of the beloved trailer.

The Tin Can Tourists were actually founded in 1919 "to unite fraternally all autocampers." An outdoor enthusiast group, they wanted to preserve clean camps and provide wholesome entertainment for campers. A soldered tin can on their radiator caps identified them as part of the group. By the 1980s the group had lost so many members that it was no longer, but was revived in 1998. Today, they exist to preserve all vintage trailers and motorhomes and are not exclusive to Airstreams.

Online there are many groups dedicated to those who love Airstreams, from Facebook pages to The Airstreamers Club, a group that exists as an online social network to bring together those who love Airstreams, both owners and non-owners.

Opposite:
The Atomium, a unique futuristic-retro structure created as the main pavilion for the 1958 World's Fair in Brussels, is the perfect companion model to another futuristic-retro structure, the Airstream.

Right: Another early 1960s marketing image of a trailerite checking out the resort island of Sveti Stefan in what was then Yugoslavia. According to Byam, "If you show people the ultimate that they can do with your product, they'll be inspired ... and buy."

Opposite top: WBCCI members still abide by Byam's main principles of living your life to its fullest, traveling with all your creature comforts, seeking out faraway lands, encouraging friendship, promoting international goodwill and making your dreams come true.

Opposite bottom: Airstreams carefully snaked though narrow mountain roads while on the Capetown to Cairo caravan. During the 1950s the trailers crossed practically every terrain that one could imagine, piggy-backing on trains, being shipped across the ocean, and driving over winding, unpaved or almost impassable roads.

The largest Airstream community can be found at www.Airforums.com. Here one can network with thousands of Airstream owners and enthusiasts. The community covers absolutely everything Airstream-related, from advice for new owners, and decorating suggestions to pop culture fun.

Another segment of the community is the magazine *Airstream Life*. This quarterly magazine, founded in 2003, is the go-to periodical regarding the world of Airstream. Articles on technical tips, human interest stories and Airstream current events and history, combined with beautiful images, make this an enjoyable, aspirational read for owners and non-owners alike. Along with Airstream, Inc., the magazine is one of the sponsors of Alumapalooza, an annual event held at Airstream's Jackson Center, Ohio factory. Part rally, part seminar, part group getaway, Alumapalooza celebrates all things Airstream and provides information, fun, tours and instruction.

Whether a group is official or not, online or off-line, these toasters on wheels certainly bring people together. Whether it's folks traveling together or a bunch of enthusiasts discussing their own Airstream dreams, the trailer is where the heart is.

THE ICON

"The dear public clasped these newfangled inventions to their hearts and started dreaming."

Wally Byam

AIRSTREAMS were popular from the very beginning, but it takes time for something to surpass the phase of "trendy" and achieve the title of "iconic." What makes a silver toaster-like home on wheels an American icon? Much like other American icons, Airstream has reached that status because it has been constant—strong, beautiful, durable, and dependable. Like Levi's, Elvis, and Coca-Cola it came on as a huge success, weathered the bad times and some questionable decades, but always remained true to Wally Byam's original vision—quality, adventure, self-reliance, innovation, hard work, community and looking good.

A cultural icon can be defined as a person or an object that represents some aspect of values, norms or ideals perceived or desired in a culture or society. One must look no further than Wally Byam's vision to see why Americans have such a soft spot for his rolling tin cans. The company's motto, "See More, Do More, Live More" could be the catchphrase for America during the postwar boom. Wally Byam created, led and personified the image of a group who rebelled, valued hard work and craftsmanship, and upon gaining some success, appreciated creature comforts. In an article in *The New York Times* (2007), Phil Patton stated, "Airstream can be seen as a symbol of the best and worst qualities of traveling Americans: the willingness to go anywhere tempered by the simultaneous wish never to leave home." The very concept of the Airstream seeps deep into the psyche of the average American, so the seed for iconic status was planted from the beginning.

Before there were recreational vehicles people realized they could use their own vehicles for camping and recreational purposes. Henry Ford, Thomas Edison, Harvey Firestone and the naturalist John Burroughs are the godfathers of RVing. Not long after the car was invented, the group, calling themselves the Vagabonds, popularized "car camping" by traveling from one

Opposite: Airstream advertising from the 1950s and 1960s held the promise of adventure with all the comforts of home. As Byam said, "If a construction area temporarily blocks your road, so what? Go into your trailer and brew up a cup of coffee, a pot of tea or take a snooze."

In 1947 famed French cyclist Alfred Letourneur demonstrated just how lightweight and easy to tow the Airstream trailer can be. The image itself demonstrates just how clever Byam was at creating a buzz and marketing his aerodynamic trailer.

camping destination to another with a caravan of automobiles, a staff and a truck outfitted as a camp kitchen. Though they slept in tents, this really was the beginning of the camping-on-wheels lifestyle.

By the time Airstreams went semi-monocoque, there were plenty of silver trailers on the market. Trailering was all the rage in the 1930s, transcontinental roads had been laid and the "US Numbered Highways" made traveling easier and more pleasant. People took to trailering for many reasons including

Though perhaps not as popular as the pink flamingo, garden gnomes are another popular choice for adding that homey touch to a trailer. Many Airstreamers adopt mascots of all kinds to travel and live with them. These kitschy items not only personalize the trailers, but they form the basis of fun stories to share with the community.

affordability, comfort, and adventure, so a trend had already been established. As interest built momentum, the war hit, eventually halting production, but also creating a need for these easy-to-move homes. Obviously, they weren't going away.

The streamlined design, though not Byam's idea, was a trend of the time and something about this look has endured. It appealed to the masses as a statement of moving forward, progress, speed, and American virility. It held the promise of rocketing into the future, into a better life. It was associated with prosperity and excitement and was closely linked to science fiction and utopian societies. This look has grown unique over time, like a classic car that has endured, which is why this particular trailer is set apart from others RVs.

Airstream could have ended with the war but endurance is another step towards becoming an American icon. Byam's tenacity paved the way for the collaboration with Curtis Wright which was essentially a life preserver for Airstream, Inc. and one step closer to his trailer reaching iconic status—weathering the bad times. In addition, his separating himself from the negative connotation of mobile homes of the time helped to keep Airstream's reputation from tarnishing.

A couple of corn-on-the-cob holders and an empty Leaning Tower of Pisa wine bottle serve as inspiration to recreate a vintage photograph of an actual Airstream at the real tower in Italy.

Advertising postcards like this one helped to inspire and feed the dream to the public. These images still work today, reminding the overburdened twenty-first century multi-tasker of a simpler, easier time.

*see the famous travel trailer featured in National Geographic

It was during the 1950s that Byam planted the seeds that started the elevation from trend to icon. In the United States that decade has been glorified; some would argue it was the best decade in American history. Postwar success created snapshots of harmony, bliss and happiness that perhaps misrepresented the experience of many Americans, but have helped

Coverage of the caravans, including the Around the World Caravan, not only served to inform and entertain those back home, but they also served as another form of wonderful PR for the company.

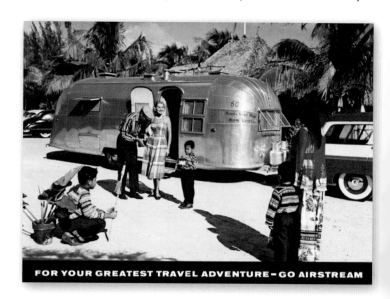

FOR YOUR GREATEST TRAVEL ADVENTURE - GO AIRSTREAM

to sear an image of "how it's supposed to be" into a nation's mind's eye. Family vacations, enjoying the good life, and safe adventure were the rewards of hard work while the concept of suburbia had folks enjoying their creature comforts. A shiny new trailer could combine all of those things, enabling you to explore, relax and be with your family as if you had never left home.

Byam put the company on the map—actually, all over the map!—with his caravans. Byam's group trips took this sense of "adventure while being comfortable" to a whole new level and his genius mastery of PR cemented Airstream's place in history. Wally stated, "I make your travel dreams come true," and he set out to prove this to the world.

Through this group travel he established the character of the Airstream owner—a smiling face with a blue beret, a modern-day explorer, seeing more and doing more than everyone else—and all from the comfort of their own homes! But the caravans were not just stunts; they showed all that could be done in a travel trailer. Images of Airstreams next to famous landmarks and with exotic people and animals were a giant "Wish You Were Here" postcard to the world. Photographs in *Life* and *National Geographic* documenting the community, a television special narrated by Vincent Price, news of Airstreamers as goodwill ambassadors … The dazzling silver cloud around Airstream wasn't just a trend; these trailers were aspirational, attainable, exploratory, comfortable; the folks were helpful and created a community. Price himself said, "A flying saucer landing could not have created more of an interest than an Airstream caravan."

The exotic locales, cool cars and happy people of vintage Airstream advertising art still make folks want to jump into the picture to soak up some of the innocent Technicolor fun.

In 1965 President Lyndon Johnson's daughter Lynda Bird Johnson toured the USA by Airstream in the "See America First" campaign. She wrote a diary about her travels called "I See America First: Diary of the President's Daughter" for *National Geographic*.

The caravans also contributed to the creation of an icon by serving as fact-finding missions for Byam, enabling him to keep improving on his already strong and sturdy product. Taking the trailers to more remote places on even more difficult terrain gave Byam a wealth of information on how to make the longest lasting, most solid trailer he could. And he did.

By the 1960s these seeds had grown strong roots with Technicolor images of happy American families doing wonderful things with their trailers.

NASA and Airstream have had a long history together. Here President Nixon visits astronauts (from left) Neil Armstrong, Michael Collins and Buzz Aldrin in their mobile quarantine unit after Apollo 11 landed back on Earth. They were kept in the Airstream for fear they carried "moon germs" from their visit. Since then, Airstreams have brought astronauts to the launchpad as they prepare for a mission.

Fishing, going to the beach, having meals in interesting places—life with an Airstream ensured happiness, limitless possibilities and a colorful life. Iconic snapshots from this time included John F. Kennedy's mobile Airstream office during a visit to New Mexico, President Lyndon Johnson's daughter Lynda Bird promoting the "See America First" campaign while touring the country in an Airstream, NASA's use of the trailer to transport astronauts to launchpads and the members of Apollo 11 chatting with President Nixon from their quarantine in a specially built Airstream after the first voyage to the moon. These images served their marketing purpose at the time but like Forrest Gump with his pictures of celebrities, they also cemented the silver trailer as an important part of history.

The late 1960s, the 1970s and the 1980s were slower times in the world of Airstreams. Air travel became easier, gas prices soared, the times were changing and trailering became quaint; eventually the connotations sank from aspirational middle-class adventure to a white trash punch line. The company itself struggled during this period as it changed hands and attempted to change with the times.

Then came the 1990s, the decade where everything came together and iconic status was reached. The history, durability and aspirational aspects

Even when parked near San Francisco's Golden Gate Bridge, trailering in an Airstream with all the comforts and luxuries of home is truly "Fifth Avenue on Wheels."

Though there are many imitators, purists demand the original Don Featherstone plastic flamingos. Although Union Plastics went out of business, the copyright and molds have been passed on and authentic birds can still be purchased.

of Airstream ownership appealed to a new generation. Purchase a vintage Airstream? Of course, the craftsmanship and durability assured that there were plenty to be found, which made them affordable to many. Fabulous design? The celebration of mid-century modern design was on the rise and Airstreams were closely tied to the retro-cool-atomic-age look. Trendy? The public's consciousness was going green and living the trailer life is extremely eco-friendly. The colorful PR images of the 1960s began to resurface, tugging at the collective love of American nostalgia and a yearning for simpler times. Yet, true to Byam's spirit, the company itself has evolved with the times, embracing the modern nostalgia with new interiors designed by architect Christopher Deam resulting in trailers that were just that— nostalgic on the outside and thoroughly modern and different on the inside. Airstream broke away from the traditionally conservative RV interior scheme of beige and brown and introduced oranges and greens to appeal to a younger audience. Celebrities began purchasing Airstreams not only to use on set, but as vacation homes or permanent residences. Television shows and movies upgraded the vehicle to cameos or starring roles *on* screen. With the 2007 introduction of an Airstream into the Museum of Modern Art, there was no longer any question—Airstream is an American icon. Airstreams are as American as apple pie, Elvis and Marilyn Monroe (and just as good looking!).

Like Marilyn and her white dress (or Chanel No. 5), Airstream has a famous prop of its own. Airstreams and pink plastic lawn flamingos go together like

Elvis and a pompadour. It is possible to live without it, but together it's just so much better. There was no clear-cut moment when Airstream owners started poking the cheerful avians next to their doors, but the rise of the flamingo started even before the trailer company.

In the pre-Disney 1920s, Florida was a popular vacation destination. Flamingos, native to the state, were an exotic discovery and pretty soon became the unofficial tourist symbol. Travelers would come home with souvenirs of the bird, status symbols that proved they were able to travel.

In 1952 Union Plastics Company introduced the first pink flamingo lawn ornament—an uninspired flat and boring concept. Next came a three-dimensinal foam version that fell apart and ended up serving as a chew toy for suburban dogs. By 1956 the company hired Don Featherstone—a twenty-one-year-old art student—to sculpt a new version. The now-famous atomic-pink birds went on sale in 1957 and became all the rage in suburban homes and gardens through the 1960s. By the 1970s the trend died out, but with the '50s revival in the 1980s (and a *New York Times* article entitled: "Where did all those (Plastic) Flamingos Go?") sales shot up and 1985 saw a record number of sales.

Featherstone never got royalties for his creation but in 1987 he was honored when the company began pressing his signature into the birds. Union Plastics went out of business in 2006, but luckily the copyright and molds were sold to a different company, so today authentic pink Featherstone flamingos are still available.

Airstreamers, considering their trailers homes even though on wheels, picked up on this suburban marker. It's not uncommon to see the birds staked in the ground near a parked Airstream as the owners' punctuation to their statement of their trailer as "home sweet home."

Many popular American companies and brands have collaborated with Airstream, including the retailer Eddie Bauer. The trailer is geared toward the more outdoorsy Airstreamer with a rear hatch providing the ability to stow light gear such as kayaks and an outdoor shower to hose them down with. Collaborations such as these further cement the Airstream brand in the public's consciousness.

THE POP CULTURE
PHENOMENON

"I have parked in Central Park in New York, at the curb on Fifth Avenue."

Wally Byam

ONCE SOMETHING is an icon, everyone wants a piece of it. Celebrities must own it, movies need to showcase it, artists are inspired by it, the masses long for it. The current state of Airstream proves that the Silver Twinkie has indeed reached icon status.

Celebrities always love the best of everything so it is no wonder they have had a long love affair with Airstream. All sorts of famous people have lived, traveled, hid out and worked in Airstream trailers. A 1937 *Popular Science* article noted that "movie actresses are employing them as dressing rooms on location." This is something that hasn't changed much over time, except that the number of trailers being used has increased!

One of the more well-known Airstream owners of recent times is Matthew McConaughey, who famously lived in an Airstream in Malibu, California, for years before building a permanent residence which could hold all three of his trailers. Other celebrities who have owned silver bullets include Gypsy Rose Lee, Tom Hanks, Johnny Depp, Lenny Kravitz, Brad Pitt, Angelina Jolie, Denzel Washington, Sandra Bullock, Patrick Dempsey, Eddie Vedder … the list goes on and on.

In 2002 Ralph Lauren outfitted and auctioned four vintage Airstreams to raise money for the Polo Ralph Lauren Foundation to benefit medically under-served persons. Jesse James of West Coast Choppers built an Airstream-themed custom motorcycle and sidecar for the "Legend of the Motorcycle" show in 2008. Pamela Anderson's all-white Lovestream was personalized to her tastes, stripper pole and all!

Airstreams have made quite the number of guest appearances on both the small and big screens. TV appearances have included shows such as: *Promised Land, The Simple Life, Heroes, Grey's Anatomy, Justified, Sons of Anarchy* and *Grimm*, to name a few. Donald Trump challenged contestants to create a mobile business using an Airstream on his show *The Apprentice* and a few seasons later

Opposite:
With appearances in film and television and a stay in the Museum of Modern Art; the trailer that *ID* magazine named one of the top ten industrial design concepts has certainly earned its spot as a pop culture icon.

Right: Airstream's notable form has been made into countless products, from jewelry to miniatures to this string of mini Airstream lights.

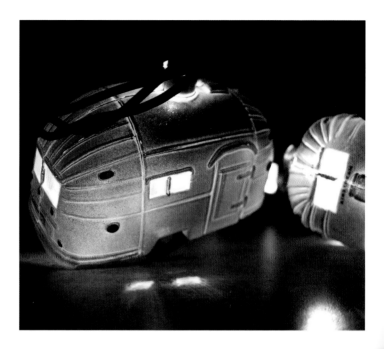

Below: The Lovestream was a gift to actress Pamela Anderson from *Playboy* editor and publisher Hugh Hefner. The all-white trailer was outfitted with *Playboy*-bunny seat cushions, a disco ball, white shag carpeting and a stripper pole.

According to Leah Gilbertson, who painted this piece, the trailers are iconic because "we have come to romanticize this Atomic Age fairytale and long for living part of that dream. In addition, there is also the lure of portable living, hitting the road and becoming a modern-day gypsy of sorts. They combine our love of mobility, adventure, home ownership and shiny things."

the trailers were used as part of the show again on the *Celebrity Apprentice*. Author and screenwriter Diablo Cody hosted a web-based talk show called the *Red Band Trailer* out of her own Airstream.

Airstreams have made many appearances on the big screen as well. A short list includes cameos in the following films: *The Long, Long Trailer, Independence Day, The Right Stuff, Wall Street 2, Charlie's Angels, Raising Arizona, What's Eating Gilbert Grape*, and *Mars Attacks*.

Besides filmmakers, other artists have been inspired by the promise and beauty of the Airstream trailer. Leah Gilberston paints over cut-up, reassembled pigment prints of photographs for stunning images of Airstreams that blur the line between photo and painting, fact and fiction. She's inspired by the streamlined profiles of Airstreams, but it's the reflective surface that really captures her imagination as "they offer distorted clues suggesting what might exist beyond edges of the painting and even behind the viewer."

Gilbertson sums up the Airstream dream:

> The attempt to reconcile our dreams of limitless possibilities and flawless facades with our more mundane struggles and complicated realities ... [I] have found that Airstreams have become a perfect vehicle for that journey, so until I'm able to own one myself I'll have to be content making paintings of them.

Airstreams have often been compared to spaceships and artist Joe Scarpa's *Port of Call: Earth* finally turned an old trailer into one!

The artist who created *Airstream Gothic*, Brad Cornelius, loves that the trailer "draws like-minded people, at rest stops and parking lots, and thumbs up as we're passing someone at 65 mph. It's a tool for connecting—sometimes in small ways, other times in larger ways—to other people like you."

Artist Paul Loughridge creates these lunchboxes from vintage aluminum Priscilla lunch pails, using wheels from an old roller skate and 35-mm film containers for propane tanks.

Brad Cornelius is a photographer and illustrator who wanted to pluck the iconic trailers from the campground and elevate them into a work of art. He created a parody of Grant Wood's *American Gothic* portraying the famed couple as beret-wearing flamingo-toting Airstreamers (well, the man at least— his wife may not totally be on board by the looks of her). "Pairing Airstreams

Once MTV takes notice, it's official that you've infiltrated the pinnacle of pop culture. Pictured here is the vintage Airstream the company housed in the lobby of their Santa Monica, California offices, complete with a patch of AstroTurf.

Below and right: The Hairstream is a full-service mobile hair salon housed in an Airstream trailer. Conversions like this would have made Byam proud—customers showing their spirit for innovation, creation and living their dreams! Other unique Airstream businesses include food trucks, mobile clothing stores and tattoo parlors.

with beloved paintings seemed only natural; a reinforcement of their status as icons." To Cornelius, they are the pinnacle of design, "so few materials and such little room adding up to something far more than the sum of its parts."

In Sacramento, California, aliens invaded an old trailer and landed in Southside Park in an art installation created by the artist Joe Scarpa. (Technically it is a 1948 Curtis Wright, but it merits inclusion as those were designed under Byam's watch.) The artist found it being used as a chicken coop. The theme of the playground was "universe," and he wanted to construct a spaceship based on the 1950s sci-fi B movies: "The aluminum travel trailers from that period were an ideal platform to work from."

Airstream conversions show the plucky spirit and creativity of the Airstreamer. They take the motto of "see more, do more" a few steps further to see *even* more and do *a lot* more. Their creativity and can-do attitude forges new paths for themselves with their trailers. Wally Byam would be impressed. From the early days of trailering, businesses immediately grabbed on to the idea of Airstreams as mobile showrooms. Companies that used them for this purpose included Kelvinator, General Electric, RCA, and Singer Sewing Machines. Doctors used them to bring the exam room to patients. Religious organizations used them in missionary work. Bookmobiles started to pop up, bringing reading materials further into communities.

Some Airstream hotels offer visitors the chance to take a step into one of Airstreams marketing images from the mid-twentieth century. The Shady Dell's Airstream (and the whole park) has a 1950s feel.

Above and opposite top: The trailers at Kate's Lazy Desert have a 1960s psychedelic vibe, similar to the styling of co-owner Kate Pierson's band, The B-52s. They were restored by artists Philip Maberry and Scott Walker, whose house is featured in The B-52s' "Love Shack" video.

During World War II Airstreams were used as housing for wartime marriages. The US Army Medical division purchased fifteen Airstream trailers as rolling hospitals. After the war they were used as housing for GI Bill students.

In more modern times, conversions have gotten even more creative. Airstreams have been used as mobile restaurants, hot-dog stands and food carts. Washington State's Hairstream houses a full-service beauty salon that's mostly stationary, but can also travel to clients for special events. New York City's Redwood Kitchenette and Bar (now closed) had an entire trailer inside the restaurant serving as its bar. New York's Lower East Side Girls' Club hoisted a vintage one up to the second floor to repurpose as a recording studio. MTV's Santa Monica office has a 1957 trailer sitting in its lobby atop AstroTurf.

Turning an old (or new) Airstream into a motel room has been gaining popularity in recent years. Many existing hotels and motels have brought in an Airstream to rent as a motel room. Even American campground chain KOA (Kampgrounds of America) have now gotten in on the action, bringing the Airstream accommodations into some of its parks.

Taking this idea one step further is the concept of "Glamping" or "glamorous camping." Glamping is for those who like the romance of camping with none of the hassle. Airstreams go hand-in-hand with this concept as the

trailer with the least "white trashy" mobile home connotation of them all. Airstreams are sleek, silver, shiny—very glamorous. Staying in an Airstream hotel gives non-owners and the curious a taste of what Airstream living is really like. The Shady Dell in Bisbee, Arizona is a vintage trailer hotel that has been around since 1927, first as an actual trailer park, then as a trailer motel.

Left: A little bit of Americana in France, BelRepayre's Airstream and Retro Trailer Park's Apollo Lounge houses a vintage Airstream that serves as a diner. The park was opened by two former circus performers with a shared love of vintage vehicles and the outdoors.

Left: The owner of the Grand Daddy hotel had a vision for an upscale trailer park, and saw no reason to keep it at ground level. After fighting those who said it was impossible, he shipped in seven trailers from the United States and used cranes to place them on the rooftop.

Above: The Grand Daddy describes their Airstreams as "over-the-top, tongue-in-cheek and always-surprising capsules of glee." Each themed trailer was designed by a different local artist.

Below: The Grand Daddy's rooftop trailer park keeps up the kitschy vibe with a rooftop bar and a movie theater appropriately called The Pink Flamingo Cinema.

In the early 2000s, it housed nine vintage travel trailers, including one 1949 Airstream, in a retro-styled community that transports visitors to back to the 1950s during their stay.

Kate Pierson of the band The B-52s first founded Kate's Lazy Meadow in the Catskill Mountain region of New York. After flooding in the area became a problem, she carefully shipped the Airstreams across the country and opened up a western outpost in Landers, California and called it Kate's Lazy Desert. Fully restored and decorated in colorful wacky themes, these trailers are like something out of a B-52s video!

Utah's Shooting Star Drive-in and Airstream Resort has a mid-century vibe with eight movie-themed trailers to rent. To cap off the retro feel, the facility has an old school drive-in theater, complete with permanently parked 1960s convertibles from which to enjoy the show. Glamping isn't just for residents of the United States. In Mirepoix, France, ten vintage Airstreams are decked out in period style ranging from the 1940s to the 1970s at BelRepayre Airstream and Retro Trailer Park. Known as Europe's first vintage trailer park, there's also an Airstream bar inside their Apollo Lounge. In Capetown, South Africa, the Grand Daddy Hotel is a swanky boutique hotel with an Airstream trailer park on the roof.

If an overnight stay in an Airstream doesn't last long enough for you, you could choose to be laid to eternal rest in your very own Airstream-for-one. The personalization of coffins is a tradition originating in Ghana, where funerals are important affairs and participants go all-out to celebrate the life lived. Precious items needed in the afterlife are presented to the deceased and buried with them. Elaborate coffins were made for tribal chiefs, carved by

The ultimate Airstream enthusiast can roll into the afterlife in his or her own Airstream coffin. Definitely one of the more unique odes to the Silver Bullet, coffins like this one are hand-crafted by a small number of skilled craftsmen in the Republic of Ghana. They are works of art.

Dorothy may have had ruby slippers to get her home, but many an Airstreamer might prefer to have a pair of these silver slippers from Vroomers so they'll always feel at home.

local carpenters who also trained apprentices. In the 1950s an apprentice carved a personalized coffin for his grandmother and a new tradition began. Being the icon that it is, naturally there is a carved Airstream coffin.

Something a little cozier to be enjoyed while kicking around in your own trailer (or pretending to) would be a pair of toasty Airstream slippers. If you can't tow an Airstream, you might as well have two carry you around *and* keep your toes warm. Clothing, jewelry and any other number of wearable Airstream art can be found a few clicks away on the internet.

Humans need not be the only ones to take part in all of the Airstream fun. The pet camper was created when designer Judson Beaumont bought his daughter a dog and she decided the dog needed his own house. Not wanting

Not wanting an ugly doghouse cluttering up his backyard, the artist behind Straight Line Designs' pet camper was inspired by Airstream's beautiful lines, iconic status and nostalgic vibe.

Left: Florida's glorious Airstream Ranch consists of eight Airstreams nose-down in the ground. It's been called an eyesore, a dumping ground, kitsch, art and a thing of beauty. Regardless, it might just be the most moving tribute to the Airstream yet.

Below: Jason Smeed's Wally Byam tattoo shows that Airstream symbolizes much more than just a cool-looking trailer. The camper with nicknames like the Silver Twinkie, the Silver Burrito and The Toaster on Wheels is really about community, friendship, living your dreams and so much more.

a stationary eyesore in the backyard, Beaumont experimented with the idea of a doghouse on wheels, starting out with pickup trucks and vans and ending up with a streamlined trailer design. His company Straight Line Designs created it out of aluminum and stainless steel.

For some, the subtle approach is the equivalent of a long, flat cornfield-bordered stretch of road. Some need to show their appreciation in a big way. Eight Airstreams buried nose down along eastbound lanes in Dover, Florida, serve as an eye-catching ode to the camper. Inspired by Cadillac Ranch in Amarillo, Texas, it is ambitious, beautiful and tugs at the emotions (What a waste! How grand! Gosh, I love Airstreams!). The brainchild of Frank Bates, owner of a nearby RV dealership, the installation was threatened when the county wanted to classify the installation as a corporate sign, junk storage or simply, an eyesore, rather than as art. Thousands of signatures were gathered to save the structure and the legal battle was won. "People drive by and they smile," Bates said. "Why wouldn't I fight to keep something like that?"

Another way to proclaim your love for something is to permanently draw it on to your own body. Something like an Airstream doesn't just lend itself to a love of design, but love of a certain lifestyle and mindset. Many have permanently etched their odes to the trailer on to their very own bodies.

After a bad accident left him disabled in his early thirties, Jason Smeed bought an Airstream. "I spent the first night in it with no intentions of making it my full-time residence but I was so comfortable that I stayed in it the next night and the next. In fact I have spent every night since then in my Airstream." He became fully immersed in the lifestyle, joining the local chapter of the WBCCI and attending various rallies. At Alumapalooza 2011 he met Airstream artist Michael DePraida, fell in love with his artwork and sought permission to reproduce DePraida's Byam portrait on his own body. Smeed added his own touch to the piece, creating a design of Airstreams circling a globe with a compass rose, to symbolize the many caravans Byam led all around the world. Adding in his WBCCI member numbers at the bottom and a fleur de lis at the top, he found tattoo artist (and fellow Airstreamer) Charon Henning to actually do the work inside his own Airstream. Why the tattoo?

According to Byam, "Adventure is where you find it, any place, every place, except at home in the rocking chair."

Most of all … I was inspired by the short time I had spent around other Airstreamers but it was also a combination of the love of the work of Michael DePraida, a love of all things Airstream and a lot of it just was simply me wanting to have a reminder of this new exciting chapter of my life that I could carry with me always. This is an Airstream tattoo like no other: drawn by two Airstreamers, tattooed by a third Airstreamer, inside of an Airstream.

PLACES TO VISIT

Airstream Factory, 419 West Pike Street, Jackson Center, Ohio 45334. Tel: (937) 596-6111. Website: www.airstream.com/company/plant-tours/

HOTELS

Shady Dell, 1 Douglas Road, Bisbee, Arizona 85603.
  Tel: (520) 432-3567. Website: www.theshadydell.com
Kate's Lazy Desert, 58380 Botkan Road, Landers, California 92285.
  Tel: (845) 688-7200. Website: www.lazymeadow.com
Shooting Star Drive-In, 2020 West Highway 12, Escalante, Utah 84726.
  Tel: (435) 826-4440. Website: www.shootingstardrive-in.com
KOA Campgrounds. Tel: (888) 562-0000. Website: www.koa.com
BelRepayre Airstream & Retro Camping, Manses 09500, Manses, France.
  Tel: +33 (0)561 68 11 99. Website: www.airstreameurope.com
The Grand Daddy Hotel, 38 Long Street, Capetown, South Africa 8001.
  Tel: +27 21 424 7247. Website: www.granddaddy.co.za

ART INSTALLATIONS

Port of Call: Earth, Southside Park, 2115 6th Street, Near U Street,
  Sacramento, California 95818
Airstream Ranch, Interstate 4, just before Exit 13, Dover, Florida

FURTHER READING

Airstream Life magazine. Website: http://airstreamlife.com
Banham, Russ. *Wanderlust: Airstream at 75*. Greenwich Publishing Group, 2007.
Burkhart, Bryan and Hunt, David. *Airstream: The History of the Land Yacht*. Chronicle Books, 2000.
Burkhart, Bryan; Noyes, Phil; Areiff, Allison. *Trailer Travel: A Visual History of Mobile America*. Gibbs Smith, 2002.
Byam, Wally; McClure, Forrest (editor); Luhr, Rich (editor). *The Byam Books: Fifth Avenue on Wheels; Trailer Travel Here and Abroad*. Church Street Publishing, 2012.
Featherstone, Don and Herzing, Tom. *The Original Pink Flamingos: Splendor on the Grass*. Schiffer Publishing Ltd, 1999.
Keister, Douglas. *Silver Palaces*. Gibbs Smith, 2004.
Littlefield, Bruce. *Airstream Living*. Harper Design, 2007.
Winick, David. *Airstreams: Custom Interiors*. Schiffer Publishing, Ltd, 2010.

INDEX

Page numbers in italics refer to illustrations